A Manual Miscellany for organ

EDITED BY
C. H. Trevor

Book Two

NOVELLO PUBLISHING LIMITED
8/9 Frith Street, London W1V 5TZ

Order No: NOV 262749

EDITORIAL NOTE

Although the pieces in this book have suggestions for registration on an organ of two (and sometimes three) manuals, all the pieces can be played effectively on a one-manual instrument with appropriate stops. The pedals can be used at the player's discretion.

As stops with the same names do not always produce the same effect on different organs, other registrations should be used if those suggested are not effective or suitable on any particular instrument. The directions for registration in brackets may be used or not at the player's discretion.

All *cresc.* and *dim.* should be made with the swell pedal and not by adding or subtracting stops. If the organ is an unenclosed one-manual, the dynamics should be ignored except where it is possible to change the registration without interrupting the flow of the music.

C.H.T.

CONTENTS

Fugue in C

Gt. light 8. 4. (2.)

Friedrich Wilhelm Zachau
(1663—1712)
teacher of Handel

E 2749

Sonata in G

Gt. Flute 8.
Sw. Diapason (or Oboe 8.)

Domenico Scarlatti
(1685—1767)

Andante con moto (♩. = about 72)

6

Introductory Voluntary

Christian Friedrich Rudolph
(1801—1829)

Gt.⎫ soft 8.
Sw.⎭
Sw. to Gt.

Chorale prelude (bicinium), "Christus, der uns selig macht"

Gt. Flutes 8. 4.
Sw. Diapasons 8. 2. (or 8. 4.)

Georg Philipp Telemann
(1681—1767)

Alternative registration:
Ch. (or Sw.) 8. 2. (or 8. 4.) both hands.

THREE SHORT PRELUDES

Johann Gottlieb Töpfer
(1791—1870)

Ch. Flutes 8. 4. (or Sw. Diapason 8.)

Andante con moto

No. 1

legato

rit.

Johann Christian Heinrich Rinck
(1770—1846)

Sw. (or Ch.) soft 8.

Adagio

No. 2

rall.

Johann Gottfried Vierling
(1750—1813)

Gt. Diapason(s) 8. 4.

Moderato

No. 3

rit.

PASTORALE

Ignace Leybach
(1817–1891)

Tambourin sur des Noëls

R.H. Gt. (or Ch.) Flute(s) 8. (4.)
L.H. Sw. Oboe (or Diapason) 8. [+ 4ft.?]

Jean Jacques Charpentier
(1734—1794)

The Swell Oboe should not be used unless it is pleasing and even in tone.

ADAGIO (K. 356)
(written in 1791 for glass harmonica)

Mozart
(1756–1791)

Sw. Flute 8. [box (half) open.]

The Swell box should be (nearly) closed for the repeats.

Chorale prelude, "Allein Gott in der Hoh sei Ehr"

Gt. 8. 4. (2.)

Johann Gottfried Walther
(1684—1748)

Prelude (Op. 89. No. 6)

Georg Goltermann
(1824—1898)

Sw. soft 8.

Diapason Movement
(from a voluntary)

Gt. Diapasons 8. 4.

William Walond
(1725—1770)

TWO PIECES

César Franck
(1822—1890)

No. 1. Grand Choeur

No. 2. Berceuse

Solo. Gt. (or Ch.) solo stop 8.
Sw. soft 8.

Andante amabile

If preferred, this piece can be played throughout on the Swell.

VOLUNTARY

Roseingrave was appointed the first organist of St.
George's Church, Hanover Square, London, in 1725.

Thomas Roseingrave
(1690 — 1766)

Diapason 8.

Largo assai

Versillo del Sexto Tono

Francisco Llissá
(early 18th century)

light 8. 4.

E 2749

TRIO

R.H. Gt. (or Ch.) Flute 8.
L.H. Sw. Oboe (or Diapason) 8.

Jean Adam Guilain
(early 18th century)

Alternative registrations:
R.H. Sw. Flutes 8. 4.
L.H. Ch. Clarinet 8. Piccolo 2. (or Flute 4.) | Ch. (or Gt.) Flute(s) 8. (4.) both hands.

Hymnus, "Pange lingua"

R.H. Sw. Diapason 8.
L.H. Gt. Diapason 8.

Guillaume Lasceux
(1740 – 1831)

Alternative registration:
R.H. Gt. light 8. 4. (2.)
L.H. Sw. Trumpet 8.

24

Prélude du Premier Ton

Gt. Diapason(s) 8. 4.

Nicolas Gigault
(1625—1707)

Noël, "Chantons je vous prie"

Sw. (or Ch.) light 8. 2. (or 8. 4.)

Nicolas le Bègue
(1630—1702)

THREE PIECES
No. 1. Chorale prelude, "Wo Gott der Herr nicht bei uns hält"

Gt. Diapasons (or Flutes) 8. 4.

Johann Pachelbel
(1653—1706)

Moderato

26

No. 2. Fugue (No. 10)
(Magnificat quinti toni)

Gt. (or Sw. or Ch.) light 8. 2. (or 8. 4.)
[or Flutes 4. 2. or Flute 4 alone.]

Allegretto

This piece can be played an octave higher with good effect on either Ch. Flutes 8. 4. or Sw. Bourdon 16. Fifteenth 2.

No. 3. Praeludium

Diapason 8.

Andante

Fughetta in G minor

Gt. Diapasons 8. 4. (2.)
Sw. Diapasons 8. 4. 2. (Mixture.) box closed.
Sw. to Gt.

Georg Andreas Sorge
(1703 – 1778)

THREE INTERLUDES

Charles Alexis Chauvet
(1837—1871)

Trumpet Voluntary

John Stanley
(1713 — 1786)

E 2749

Made in England